Edward King 1862–1951

The Portsmouth Painter who Influenced Van Gogh

John M Haggarty

TRICORN
BOOKS

Edward King 1862-1951
The Portsmouth Painter who Influenced Van Gogh
John M Haggarty

Design © 131 Design Ltd
www.131design.org
Text © John Haggarty

ISBN 978-0-9573435-2-8

A CIP catalogue record for this book is available
from the British Library.

Published 2012 by Tricorn Books,
a trading name of 131 Design Ltd.
131 High Street, Old Portsmouth,
PO1 2HW

www.tricornbooks.co.uk

Images by kind permission:
The Bridgeman Art Library
Portsmouth Museum and Records Service
The Witt Collection at the Courtauld Institute of Art
Van Gogh Museum, Amsterdam (Vincent van Gogh Foundation)

Printed & bound in UK by Berforts Group Ltd

Contents

Dedicated to my mother, Annie Brady-Haggarty, 1912-2007.

'Since, thy gay morn of life overcast, Chill came the tempest's lour;
And ne'er Misfortune's eastern blast did nip a fairer flower.' (RB)

Note from the Author

Since starting to research this book all I have been able to see of Edward King's work is a few of his Blitz paintings, all painted during his incarceration in the Portsmouth Lunatic Asylum; almost all 83 of his recorded paintings are in Portsmouth's City Museum.

I would like to thank the Courtauld Gallery in London where I was able to get photocopies of his early newspaper lithographs e-mailed to me within two hours of contacting them, and who waved reproduction fees for this book.

Encouraged by their professionalism, I was determined to dig deeper and try to find some of Edward King's earlier work. On an obscure website I found three paintings entitled: *Girls Dancing in a London Street, Tug of War at Saint Ives* and *Street Leading to Woodland,* and one of unnamed children playing by the seashore also at Saint Ives, circa 1881/1882.

I was astounded by these paintings and by his colour palette; the movement he has instilled in the children is magical. Edward King has made this project very worthwhile.

Introduction

Edward King his life and work 1883-1924

Genre painter & illustrator, began contributing to the *ILN* 1883 – [*Illustrated London News*]

He treated both rural and metropolitan subjects in a new and realistic way, giving through sensitive drawing and minute hatching, a sympathetic view of poor Londoners and country folk. He was one of the artists much admired by Van Gogh. Contributed to *ILN* [1883-87]; *The Pall Mall Magazine*; *Punch* [1905].[1]

I bought an issue of the London News – because of a sheet by King - Workmen in a carriage of the Underground Railway. (Vincent van Gogh)

Which must have reminded Van Gogh of his own journey by Underground when returning from a visit to the Gladwells' at Lewisham on 18 November 1876 (*LT* 82), as well as of Doré's drawing of the Underground Railway (cited in *LT* 84. 21 January 1877).

Vincent often bought a single issue simply for a specific drawing it contained. It was in this way that

[1] Houfe, Simon 1978, *The Dictionary of 19th Century British Book Illustrators*, Antique Collectors Club, Suffolk.

he acquired King's *The Workman's Train* in April 1883.

You write about a beautiful sheet in The Graphic *by Howard Pyle.* [1853-1911, American illustrator, who founded an art college in the US].

If you mean a composition that reminds one of the Terborch or Nicholas Keyzer, Pen and the Colonist's — yes, I was struck by it too, so much so that I have ordered the issue. Yes, it is a damned fine thing. I bought an issue of the London News for the same reason, because of a sheet by King — Workmen in a Carriage of the Underground Railway.

There is something stimulating and invigorating, like old wine about those striking, powerful, virile drawings.[2] (R23 c20 January 1883)

I first became aware of Edward King and his work purely by accident. I was showing my grandchildren around an exhibition of pre-war children's toys at the Portsmouth City Museum, when I literally stumbled across two of King's Blitz paintings. It was these strikingly evocative paintings, full of light and colour, that initially took my interest; after reading the descriptive plaque on the wall that stated the painter of these works, Edward King, had spent most of his adult life, the period from 1926 until his death in 1951, in the Borough of Portsmouth Lunatic Asylum, I was intrigued. Why, I wondered? What

[2] *The Complete Letters of Vincent van Gogh*, 1978, Vol.iii, Thames & Hudson Ltd, London

had happened for him to end up in such a place? I decided to try to find out.

After doing a little research on King, I discovered that he had been an illustrator for some of the most prestigious news magazines of his day and an impressionist painter; that he had exhibited not only at the Royal Academy but also at the most prestigious galleries both here and abroad. I had hoped to find a clue to this through further research by finding out about his incarceration in the mental hospital and by tracking down anything that was known about him.

It was then that I ran into difficulty. At first it appeared that very little was known, and even less recorded, about Edward King in any biographical, historical or artistic sense. I found out that although Portsmouth City Museum does have some information of that period of King's life, it is almost all anecdotal. These details and information only came to light when the City Museum decided, in 1984, to have an exhibition in conjunction with the local newspaper, *The Portsmouth Evening News*, called *Home Front: Images of Portsmouth 1939-45*, about the people of Portsmouth during the Second World War. They wanted to include some of King's Blitz paintings in the exhibition so they placed an article in *The Portsmouth Evening News* asking for information from anyone who had any of his work or information about him.

Information came mainly from letters to the City Museum from former staff at the asylum, local people who had met King on his painting expeditions, or a few King cognoscenti who had gleaned some details from him about his early life before he was confined to the asylum.

Details about Edward King's incarceration in the asylum, from 1926 until his death in 1951, are also very sketchy as all his records are 'closed' for 100 years, (as are all mental health records). Still, I decided to approach St James' Hospital with a view to getting access to Edward King's records and to try and put some meat on the bare bones of his life. Unfortunately this has been refused; the reason given is that it would be not be practicable for me to anonymise any information, with which I must agree.

I had a contact in the City Museum, Stephen Brookes, the Military History Officer; I had catalogued a collection of D-Day photographs for him. When I mentioned to Stephen that I was thinking of using Edward King, purely on the basis of his two paintings I had seen in the Museum, for my monograph, he lent me a commemorative book of the paintings by local artists detailing the Nazi Blitz of their four cities, Portsmouth, Exeter, Stalingrad and Caen. This book, *Du Sang et des Larmes*, (Blood and Tears) had been the inspiration of Conseil Général Du Calvados and was published in 1994. He also told me that the City Museum had a small file on King in the Museum's Records Office.

It was the file in the Museum's Records Office office that I found fascinating; the letters from many people who had known Edward King or knew someone who had known him, or had worked at the hospital when he was there. The contents of these letters were a source of wonder and puzzlement to me, especially when I found a rough memo written on a scrap of paper to Stella Benham, the Senior History Curator of the City Museum, in 1984, from a Professor Hutchinson of Yale University, a distant relative of King. Hutchinson asserted that King had been an important influence on Vincent van Gogh and was mentioned in a book in the Center for British Art in Yale University to that effect: according to the file, it appeared this memo had not been followed up.

I decided I would follow my old school motto 'nil sine labore' and follow up Hutchinson's memo.

So very little is known of this artist, states Professor Ronald Pickvance, speaking for the Fine Arts Department of Nottingham University and the Arts Council of Great Britain. He then goes on to quote from a letter written by one of the most famous artists the world has ever known, Vincent van Gogh, who categorically states that this English artist influenced his work.

I must admit I was a bit taken aback when I read Professor Pickvance's comment. Is there really not much known about Edward King? Could an artist, capable of painting such beautiful pictures of the ruined buildings of Old Portsmouth, really be so inconsequential? I want to show that there is very much known about this artist, and that his work ranks with the very best of his contemporaries.

According to King's daughter, Una, he was an accomplished artiste in music and in painting. His talents ranged from playing first violin in Sir Henry Wood's famous concert orchestra, to creating the 'mood' music for the silent cinema of the day, to having fairly comprehensive entries in all the great Art Dictionaries, and being plauded by the French equivalent of the Royal Academy.

The most difficult parts of this enigma to research are the years that King spent in the lunatic asylum. Even though he was denied the freedom to associate with his contemporaries and therefore was unable to expand in his art for all those years, he still eventually managed to produce beautiful and stimulating paintings up until just two weeks before his death. The quality and variety of his work is a testimony to a true master of his craft.

Outline Chronology

1862	Born 11th December, Kensington, London.
1876	Father deserts the family and orders them out of house.
1876	Sent to Leipzig to study violin under Schradieck.
1878	Returns to England and takes up painting.
1879	Exhibits his first big painting at the International Exhibition, Crystal Palace.
1879/1884	Both Edward and his brother Gunning King live a Bohemian life.
1883/1887	Contributing to the ILN, Punch, Graphic, Pall Mall. (Van Gogh sees and buys The Workman's Train).
1885	Gunning King moves to South Harting, Edward joins him.
1886	Commissioned to paint Amelia Emilie Shipley, (future wife).
1887	Leaves for New York, due to scandal about affair.
1888	Returns from New York to marry Amelia Emily Shipley.
1888/89	Joins The New English Art Club.
1889/1904	Travels around the West Country painting

	and joins the Plein–Air movement in St Ives.
1904/1924	Has 54 paintings exhibited in the Royal Academy.
1925	Resides at 9 The Riverbank, East Moseley, Surrey.
1925/26	Wife committed to hospital; dies of Consumption (TB). Edward committed to Borough of Portsmouth Lunatic Asylum.
1940	23rd October Gunning King dies at South Harting. (Estate valued at £6,083. 1s 8p).
1941	Commissioned to paint Blitz of Portsmouth.
1948	Changed from private to National Health Service patient.

Edward King suffered a stroke and died on the 27 February 1951 in St James' Hospital, Milton Portsmouth. He was buried, at his request, in Putney Vale Cemetery, London, alongside his wife, Emilie, whom he always called 'Lovie.'

Chapter 1
King's Influence on Van Gogh

How much of an influence was Edward King on Vincent Van Gogh? Well, by comparing just one of Van Gogh's early sketches from 1881, the *Young Peasant with a Sickle,* with King's later illustrations, it could be argued that Edward King's lithographs and drawing technique had a very strong influence on him. This early drawing of Van Gogh's, although technically excellent, is a stark plain figure without any real form, depth or life.

On more than one occasion Van Gogh was forced to admit,

> *When I was in Brussels, I tried to find employment with some lithographer, but was rebuffed everywhere. I asked there for any kind of work, as I only wanted to see something of lithography and especially to learn. But they didn't want people like that.* (JH 257 6-8 November 1882)

> *What is drawing? How does one learn it? It is working through an invisible iron wall that seems to stand between what one feels and what one can do.* (JH 222 22 October 1882). [The *ILN* also turned him down]

Yet in 1884, just a year or so after he had seen and

bought King's *The Workmen's Train* he produced *The Weaver: The Whole Room Looking Right* 1884, one of his earliest attempts to create light, shade and depth using the cross-hatching technique. But it is his lithograph of *The Potato Eaters,* 1885, one of Van Gogh's best-known early works, that shows just how much of an influence King's *The Workmen's Train* was, not only in the wonderful play of light and shade on the faces of the characters, but in the whole construction of the picture. In King's lithograph *The Workman's Train,* the central fifth figure has been added as a *repoussoir*[3]; he also appears to be in the process of just sitting down, perhaps to add movement to the work and to give emphasis to the reflected light and to give the whole composition a better balance.

Incidentally, close focus, nearness of vision, attention to detail and the integration of the figures within their surroundings were all qualities that King excelled at. As in the figure of the man lighting his pipe, the flare of the match and the puff of smoke is magical: compare this with Van Gogh's feeble attempt to show the steam rising from the cup of the figure on the right in *The Potato Eaters.* Van Gogh's lithograph was originally designed with four figures and was a simple sketch, basically a study of chiaroscuro, but in his final study Van Gogh not only added a fifth figure, but also made this figure a repoussoir, and by doing so he brought the whole focal point

[3] a figure or object in the extreme foreground: used as a contrast and to increase the illusion of depth.

The Workmen's Train Edward King 1884 The Witt Collection at
the Courtauld Institute of Art

Vincent van Gogh (1853 - 1890) *The Potato Eaters*, 1885-04 Nuenen
oil on canvas, 82 x 114 cm Van Gogh Museum, Amsterdam (Vincent
van Gogh Foundation)

forward, changed the meal time from day to evening and, by showing the lamp lighted, he highlighted the reflected light onto the left cheek of the figure. There is even a suggestion too of movement from Van Gogh's new central fifth figure as she points her fork at the potatoes. This figure not only bears a striking facial resemblance to King's figure but the whole posture and focus is the same. In his cross-hatching, a characteristic of all of King's drawings with their simplicity of outline and successive, horizontal pencil strokes across the form of the subject and strong vertical lines to indicate shadows, Van Gogh has given depth, feeling and power to what was originally a rather stilted drawing.

It has been suggested that this lithograph and the subsequent painting by Van Gogh of *The Potato Eaters*, was influenced by Charles de Groux's (1867-1930) painting, *La Bénédicité*, but although de Groux was another artist and lithographer much admired by Van Gogh, de Groux's work was mainly of religious and historical subjects, whereas, in both Edward King's and Van Gogh's compositions they are depicting labourers 'reaping the fruits of their labour': the workman his train ride, the peasants their potatoes. It is King's sure instinct for form, his strength of conception, his mastery of cross-hatching and the execution of his drawings that all lead me to the conclusion that this work, and possibly many others of Van Gogh, were heavily influenced by Edward

King. These four other drawings by King, *The Old Firm: Established 1840,* and *The Wastrels, The Orange-Woman,* and *The Londoners* reinforce my argument, as they are superb examples of composition, cross-hatching, and the powerful emotion King embodies, both as an illustrator and social commentator.

Van Gogh himself confirms this, I believe, in a letter to his brother Theo, only two months after he had bought King's *The Workman's Train.* He remarked,

> *... I adopted the manner of some English artists, without thinking of imitating them, but probably because I am attracted to the same kinds of things in nature.* (*LT* 294, mid June 1883)

I feel Van Gogh is not being entirely honest in this remark to Theo; in his use of 'manner' he may be dissembling, because if he is not actually 'imitating' them, then he is certainly utilising their techniques.

Chapter 2
The Early Years

Edward King was an English artist in Portsmouth in the 1940s. Known for his Blitz paintings. He went mad.

This seems to be the sum total of the common knowledge of the Impressionist painter and illustrator, Edward King, and it does not do him justice. King was held to be a painter of great talent in his early years and is one of the most intrinsically interesting painters of the past hundred years or so. This is due in part to his wonderful illustrations in all of the most important journals of his day; *The Graphic, Illustrated London News, Pall Mall Magazine* and *Punch* to mention just a few. King's illustrations, among many others of course, are one our most useful sources for the social history of Victorian life and fortunately, most of them are well catalogued in the most prestigious of galleries and exhibitions.

The sheer volume and quality of King's work in these early years attest to his being an important artist. If the number of commissions for portraits he was getting, and the charges he was making for his work is any guide to go by, he was making a good living from his work. See appendice (h).

Some of King's contemporaries at this time were Boyd Houghton, Charles Keene and Aubrey Beardsley, all illustrators for the same publications as King, and as these publications were renowned for the quality of their artists, then surely King was, at the very least, as good an artist as these now acknowledged masters.

In King's circle were also founder members, if not the inspirational leaders, of many of the Impressionist movements springing up among the artistic communities in Britain in the latter part of the nineteenth century. King was part of this nomadic movement, as his many gallery entries show he was travelling around the south east, west and north of England. He joined the New English Art Club, an art society founded 1886; its members, most of whom were influenced by Impressionism, included one of the founding members, Philip Wilson Steer, as well as John Singer Sargent, Augustus John, Paul Nash, William Rothenstein, and Walter Sickert. The aim of this club was to secure better representation for younger painters than was available through the Royal Academy. This must have been successful for King as he had about a dozen or so of his paintings exhibited in the Royal Academy around this period. Later, King flirted with the Plein-Air movement in St. Ives, an artists' colony founded by Walter Sickert and James McNeil Whistler, where he is known to have concentrated on painting small seascapes.

To say that King was an Impressionist painter is not too difficult to justify, although I have been unable, (as yet!), to see any of his early work, other than his lithographs, and the one print of his painting offered for sale by Sothebys. (See appendix I). However, it would be fair to state that as King was involved in, and part of, these very influential groups of artists and movements, at a time when British art was going through a transition period, he was more likely than not to have been just as much an Impressionist painter as his contemporaries.

Edward King, his elder brother Gunning, and his sister were born of middle-class parents in Kensington, London. His father was a bank manager and keen amateur painter. When Edward was about fourteen years old his father left his mother, adding to the trauma a few weeks later by writing to her to 'quit the house'; this may have been the last time Edward and his brother had any contact with her or their sister. I was fortunate in my research to have access to many letters containing a wealth of detail about Edward King's life, but the two following are by far the most interesting, as both give a detailed account of his early life.

In a letter to a Mrs. Largeaut, dated 5 March 1954, King's daughter Una writes,

Edward King was born in London on December 11th 1862.

He painted from the age of five. When he was fourteen his father wanted him to join his bank. Edward King viewed this with horror and from that time he kept himself by selling his watercolours to an artists' colourman in the Tottenham Court Road for 5/- each – 2/6 in cash, 2/6 in materials. Also at this time he played violin in the Covent Garden Orchestra; all his life his two talents (painting & music) pulled against each other.

At fifteen he was discovered by a rich man who took him to Leipzig, where he studied violin under Schradich. [Schradieck, Heinrich Carl Franz 1846-1918, Teaching at the Leipzig Conservatory 1874-1882, founder of a modern violin teaching method.]

On returning to England some fifteen months later, instead of being brought out as a boy prodigy, he merely said, "I must paint." The following year he had his first big canvas hung in the Royal Academy, which was painted outside Harting church, and was called The Christening. The only training he ever had was three months at Academie mie Julian in Paris, where he got a special recommendation for his life drawings. As a young man he spent three months in New York, where he drew for Harpers Magazine. In later life he once again returned to the violin, and played for two seasons in the Queen's Hall Orchestra. Sir George Clausen was a great friend of his.[4]

---

[4] Sir George Clausen RA, (1852-1944) Professor of Art, Royal Academy 1906. Edward probably met him at the *Academie mie Julian*, an informal art school in Paris. Clausen's best known work is *Youth Mourning* 1916. Also around this period, a young Pierre Bonnard was 'moonlighting' at the Academie from his studies as a lawyer.

Mary Greenwood, administrator at St. James' writes,

His father painted as a hobby and each year they would go to a stuffy little cottage near the sea at Eastbourne; they would go sketching and make elaborate notes about colours and on their return to London would paint pictures from their sketches.

When their father left their mother the boys were sent to Leipzig to study; the mother and sister departed from his life.

Edward had no formal training and was against art schools like the Slade, but may have had a few lessons there. He had a patron, a rich fishmonger, who paid him a regular wage in return for a certain number of paintings; he also drew for Punch occasionally.

His wife was in a private lunatic asylum, and she died there in the 1920s; he was originally kept in there too and it was an agreement between his daughter and Dr Beaton for him to be transferred to St. James'.[5]

As Gunning King is known to have studied at the Slade, South Kensington Art School and at the Royal Academy, it is reasonable to suppose that Edward may have spent some time studying at these schools also; a fair assumption given that Edward's body of work around this time was being exhibited in the same galleries as Gunning's. It is also said that they were leading a Bohemian life around this period;

[5] Mary Greenwood, August 1984, Letter, Portsmouth Museum Records Office.

although we do not have any real evidence of this it is still possible to envisage it. If one looks at both Edward and Gunning's body of work for this period, it will be seen that they were leading a nomadic existence all over the south west of England and the London area. This is very evident by looking through Edward's diary entries between 1884 and 1906; he lists paintings from London, Sussex, Hampshire, Dorset, Devon, Cornwall, Wales and Yorkshire. Mary Greenwood also mentions this Bohemian period of King's life; in her letter she recalls,

> ... *they were then aged about 19 and 17, and for the next few years lived a somewhat Bohemian life, reminiscent of Du Maurier's Trilby.*

This was information she could only have got from King, because by this time she had become King's confidante, as her letter reveals, and Edward seemed to take to her.

King first exhibited at the International Exhibition at Crystal Palace where he was awarded a Bronze medal for his small oil, *Old Chelsea and the River*. He also exhibited many times between 1888 and 1924 at the Royal Academy, and although his work sold well, he was never accepted as a member.

President Fleury, the President of the Paris Salon, the direct counterpart of the Royal Academy in France, writing in the arts magazine *Revue Moderne* in 1912, criticised the R A for not admitting King. He said,

If he had been born in France, France would have given him the honours he deserved.[6]

Edward and his brother Gunning, moved to South Harting, a village on the Hampshire/West Sussex borders, in the latter part of 1884. They initially rented a property called Rock Cottage in the village for 2/6 a week, but soon moved to Lane Cottage near the Post Office, a much larger property that they were able to convert part of into a studio.[7] While both of them painted and travelled up to London to sell their work, Edward was also supplementing their income with his violin, and in some very diverse ways, from playing music for the silent movies that were all the vogue at that time, to playing the more serious stuff at Lyons Restaurant in the Strand, and still performing the Promenade Concerts with Sir Henry Wood.

Sir Henry Wood recalls in his autobiography, written shortly after the death of his first wife, the Russian Princess Olga Ouroussoff in February 1910,

I drowned at least part of my sorrow in painting and now took regular lessons from Edward King.[8]

[6] Christie, John. August 1998, *Hampshire County Magazine*, Vol. 38.
[7] Aileen List. September 1984, Psychiatric Social worker, extract from recorded interview with Stella Benham, Portsmouth Museum Records Office.
[8] Wood, Sir Henry. 1938, *My Life in Music*, Victor Gollancz London.

In 1912, Wood's wife exhibited fifty oil paintings at the Piccadilly Arcade.

Edward reminisced to Mary Greenwood,

> *After a day's painting I would eat bread and cheese, and taking up my violin I would stand back and examine my picture, playing gently the while.*
>
> *What a perfect memory, he was considered genteel and quite harmless.*[9]

This sentimental homily seems rather at odds with Edward's deriding of Gunning's work, calling him a 'chocolate box painter' and castigating him for his 'romanticised version of country life' and his commercialisation. Gunning had a long association with Bibby's, the agricultural and soap supplier; he illustrated most of their advertisements. Two of Gunning King's paintings can be seen in St. Peter's Church, Petersfield and the other in the Methodist Church in South Harting, depicting religious themes of *The Fishermen* and *The Crucifixion*.

---

9 Ibid Mary Greenwood

Chapter 3
Scandal

Edward King lived and worked in the surrounding areas of Portsmouth until he was committed to the Borough of Portsmouth Lunatic Asylum as a private patient, in a 'Withdrawn and Unresponsive state' in late 1926, amid some controversy. It was said that his daughter Una, a friend of Dr Beaton, the Superintendent,

> ... *had conspired to have him committed, so she could have control of his finances.*[10]

Which may have been quite substantial, as he was such a prolific painter and his work sold well. (See appendix H)

In about 1900, when he was living at South Harting, he was commissioned by a London barrister called Hudson to paint his wife Emily's portrait. (Amelia Emily Hudson (née Shipley) was the eldest daughter of Alexander & Amelia Shipley, (nee Burge), a mother of three children and a descendant of a political refugee from Italy, Count Antonio Demezzi of Turin. Miss Hutchinson, a great niece of hers says,

---

[10] Eleanor Traynor, Social worker, 1984, Letter, Museum Records Office

My mother told my sister that today Emily would be described as highly sexed.[11]

When Edward was 24 and living in Harting, he was commissioned to paint a portrait of the young wife of a barrister who lived in the neighbourhood with her three children, while her husband worked in London. A love affair ensued with the resultant scandal and divorce. Edward departed for Chicago, [His daughter Una writes in her letter that he also went to New York and as Harpers Weekly was based in that city and as he is known to have done a number of illustrations for Harpers around this time we must assume that either Edward or Mary Greenwood is mistaken about Chicago] and he remained there during the divorce proceedings and when all was accomplished he returned to England and married the lady.[12]

This 'scandal' is referred to in the Professor Hutchinson memo, where he says,

His Aunt Emilie married a Judge, Mr Shipley, they had two children, then ran off with King, the Bohemian painter and had other children.

Edward and Emily eventually settled in Surrey and are recorded in the Register of Electors in the Parish of East Molesey, on 25 October 1925 as residing at 9 The Riverbank, East Molesey. Edward's entry carries

---

[11] Phyllis Loe, Matron, (1940-1960), 2nd August 1984 letter/interview Stella Benhem, Museum Records Office

[12] Miss DM Hutchinson, 23 October 1984, Letter, Museum Records Office

the prefix SJ, this meant that he was a 'property owner' and had a 'substantial income' so he qualified to be called on to adjudicate in the more complex court cases.

King's wife later had to be committed to Horton Hospital, a mental institution near Epsom, as a private patient, and is supposed to have died there from Tuberculosis in early 1926. Edward was also admitted to this asylum for a short period before being transferred to The Borough of Portsmouth Lunatic Asylum later in the same year.[13]

---

[13] Ibid. Mary Greenwood Letter

Chapter 4
Committed to Asylum

The regime at St James' Asylum would have been similar to many asylums of the day,

> *Patients were kept under lock and key, and so were their visitors in the 20s, [In much the same way visitors are today in our prisons one imagines] patients were behind bars and wore grey uniforms, overcrowding was so bad that the patients had to retire to their beds immediately after their meal in the evening because of their numbers. The patients lined up behind their places at the table and removed their socks and shoes, when they had removed all their outer clothing and placed it neatly on top of the table they went up the stone staircase to the ward; the beds were so close together they had to get into them from the foot.[14]*

King's life in St James' would have been claustrophobic; the degrading physical conditions and his debilitating mental health would have plunged him into a deep feeling of loneliness, without stimulation, which to a free spirit like King must have been anathema; and in his withdrawn and unresponsive condition it may not have been too long before he became 'institutionalised.' Some of the elements of this institutionalisation are laid out

---

[14] Ibid. Phyllis Loe, Interview

by Goffman above, so one must take the interview and letter written below of King '*being most skillfully encouraged to paint again solely by the efforts and encouragement of the staff*', as perhaps wishful thinking on their part. We don't know what sort of treatment King had been undergoing; it could well be that a previous form of treatment was discontinued or perhaps it was effective or perhaps even a new kind of therapy was tried that was successful. We will not know until his medical records are available to be studied in 2051.

Extract from a transcript of a recorded interview with Councillor Phyllis Loe on 2 August 1984, by Stella Benham, Assistant Keeper of Local History, Portsmouth City Museum:

S.B. *When were you at St. James' asylum?*
P.L. *Well, I was Matron there from 1940 and remained there for almost twenty years -----*
S.B. *And you knew Teddy King?*
P.L. *I knew him well.*
S.B. *When did he begin painting? When was he encouraged to paint?*
P.L. *Well, he was admitted with profound depression, superimposed on a system of delusion, largely emanating from what he considered the origin of the world, and the contents of the Bible. It was very complex, and the staff, medical and nursing, tried very hard to alleviate the depression, which they did most skilfully by encouraging him first to draw; and gave him suitable paper and*

sketching books, pencils and charcoal etc. After a while he did; the first drawings he did were of supreme skill but most bizarre content – everything was disconnected. There was a fish in one corner, a leaf half way down and a hand. It meant nothing to me; it didn't mean anything at all; but the execution of it was obviously very skilful.

Later they encouraged him to do portraits; he asked if he could have some oils. He got those through our occupational therapy department; he always had to have a big supply of light red paint, which he said was essential for his paintings.

S.B. I believe you said he went to the Slade School of Art? P.L. He was trained there at the Slade School of Art with Sickert. He said of Sickert, 'I knew Sickert would never be any good as an artist, Sickert can't draw! Unless you can draw you can't paint.'[15]

Mrs Aileen List, a physchiatric social worker remembers,

There was a well-known patient who helped to improve both his own and other patients' surrounding; Edward King was a fine artist whose works have often been shown in the City. When he first came to the City he was a prolific painter, but when he was admitted to the hospital he lost all inclination to paint. With the encouragement of staff he started to take an interest again. Fortunately his old skills were only dormant and he soon began to produce some lovely pictures.

---

[15] Goffman, Erving. 1961, Asylums, Penguin Books Ltd., Middlesex

Edward King painted a great many works showing the results of the bombing in the last war, in this way he has provided a lasting record of that time. There was no sign of lack of concentration, whatever his problem was it did not impede his considerable talent. His paintings are beautifully executed with fresh, lively colours. They hung for a long time in the hospital and now can often be seen in the City museum.[16]

Miss DM Hutchinson in a letter to Dr John Steadman, 23 October 1984, tells of her sister, (a psychiatric social worker) on meeting Dr Beaton at a conference, introducing herself to him as a relative of Edward King. Beaton is said to have remarked,

He is as mad as a hatter, but he is a jolly good painter, so we keep him supplied with paint and canvasses; and he is perfectly happy.

King ignored Beaton and treated him with contempt, deigning to not even answering his 'Good Mornings'.
(Mary Greenwood)

Extract from transcript of a recorded interview by Stella Benham with Frank Bloxham on 1 August 1984,

S.B. *Mr Bloxham you were the head therapist at St James' Hospital?*

---

[16] Milton Memories 1995 WEA Publications, Southampton, page 20

F.B. I went there in '34. I know he's done a lot of the locks and the hospital generally and they are usually hardboard. Canvas wasn't supplied just at his whim, as it were, it was only supplied for a definite object and that was the war paintings. Occupational Therapy started around 1942.[17]

I feel it is important to try to get these facts correct because it appears that the hospital administration was either unaware of King's prominence as an artist or they were very blasé about it. If one examines the City Museum's records of King's Blitz paintings, it will show that they are described as being oil on wood.

John Christie, another King cognoscenti, who I have referenced earlier, has a number of King's paintings, one of which has two different works painted on opposite sides of a piece of cardboard. Another painting of Milton Locks shows that the painting was done on a piece of oblong 'as found' cardboard, and two paintings, which I will mention later, were also painted on cardboard.

People who met him on his painting expeditions mention that as early as eight-thirty in the morning he could be seen making his way to his chosen site, and that he often didn't bother going back for his mid-day meal, instead relying on his many friends in the area to provide for him, only returning to the ward at dusk. Incidentally he would get very annoyed if

[17] Ibid. Phyllis Loe, Interview

someone moved a boat or any other object in a scene he was painting and would insist they replaced it in the position he had last seen it,[18] true to his Plein-Air, Impressionist method.

His reasons for agreeing to the Lord Mayor of Portsmouth's wife, Margaret, Lady Daly, to paint the Blitz pictures may have been part of this longing to escape his claustrophobic environment. The Lord and Lady Mayoress may have had their own ulterior motives for supplying some of King's artists' materials as they both had full-length portraits of themselves done by King in about 1943 and some of his landscapes, as did various other city and hospital officials.

His Blitz period, 1940/41, resulted in over 40 recorded paintings, most of which are spread throughout various council departments, the City Art Gallery and private owners. Even a local public house, the Ship Inn at the Junction of Fratton Road and Church Road, in 1959 had a King painting on display. The two Blitz paintings that started me off on this venture, *High Street* and *Penny Street* can be seen in the *Portsmouth Remembered* section of the City Museum. One of his larger Blitz paintings, *Commercial Road,* is situated in the staircase of the new Police Station in Eastney Road and if you ask the duty officer, he will be glad to show it to you.

18 Ibid. Mrs Aileen List, Letter

St James' Hospital has retained a number of King's landscapes and seascapes, as well as a few of his Blitz paintings and they can be viewed by contacting the hospital administration.

King continued to paint, particularly self-portraits, the grounds of the hospital and the surrounding area on any 'canvas' he could find. He painted many portraits of his local 'patrons', for that is what many of them had become, by supplying him with artists' materials. Mary Greenwood, Frank Thompson and many others have mentioned in their letters the paintings and portraits King had done not only of them but also of the local residents in the Milton Creek area, on bits of cardboard, old asbestos sheets, pieces of wood washed up on the shores near the hospital and even using both sides of his finds occasionally.[19]

Indeed, often the size and shape of the material, the colour and type of paint he managed to scrounge from boat owners dictated the content of the painting. Many of his paintings around the Milton Locks foreshore are of all types of different craft and are painted to conform to the very shape and size of his 'canvas' – all very reminiscent of the small seascapes he painted in much earlier times during his Plein-Air period in Cornwall I should imagine.

---

[19] Frank Bloxam, 1st August 1984, Interview with Stella Benham

Chapter 5
Bomb Sites and Ruins

Previously to his being incarcerated his paintings were highly valued. One only has to look at his early gallery valuations to see this, one painting alone, *A Summer Afternoon* (1888) was offered for sale at £200.00, a very large sum in those days. Yet it is in King's Blitz paintings that you are made aware of just how great an Impressionist artist he was. His choice of palette and perspective, long thought to be neglected by the Impressionist movement, is excellent. He is deliberately sparing in his use of people or vehicles in his work, and when they are present they are used only to give depth and perspective; there are no ambulances, no fire engines, no broken bodies. There is no propaganda value in King's Blitz paintings, they are a pure study of light and shade brought to life with hot ochre and flaming reds.

The Conseil Général Du Calvados put King's Blitz paintings in context when he wrote in his foreword to King's entry in *Du Sang et des Larmes,*

His paintings pare away the superficial until only the essential remains, and may even require the reality of a pure form which can become a universal symbol. This emotion is its message, even if the work of art does have a documentary value it is most of all of psychological interest.[20]

Yet all his paintings, his portraits, seascapes and landscapes, have all been greatly undervalued. None, as far as I have been able to ascertain, have been exhibited by any museum or gallery, other than Portsmouth City Museum and its twinned city Caen. If one looks at King's paintings now, Seventy years after he painted them, one can only marvel and grieve for those lost years when he could arguably have been doing his best work. Their beauty and clarity still stand out as a testament to a painter of the first order. Who knows? If he had been allowed to develop in his art, would he have been recognised as a major talent as fêted as any of his contemporaries, such as Philip Wilson Steer (1860-1942), one of the founding members of The New English Art Club, which both Edward and Gunning joined, or Walter Sickert (1860-1942) or Max Liebermann (1847-1935)?

Why these beautiful paintings have not received much wider acclaim is difficult to understand. It is not as if they were a new form of art, or even a forgotten genre. The painting of ruins, is a classical form of art that reached its height in the second half of the eighteenth century.

---

[20] bid. Goffman Asylum page 171

Rock Cottage

The Workman's Train

Edward R Kim

The Old Firm

Oil painting on canvas by Edward R King entitled 'Oyster Street' 1941

'Girls dancing in a London street'

Oil painting on canvas by Edward R King entitled 'St. Paul's Road and St. Paul's Church' dated 1941-1943

Conclusion

When I first stumbled across this extraordinary artist's work in the Portsmouth City Museum, I thought he would make an ideal subject for a research article, based on his Blitz paintings and what Old Portsmouth looked like before the Nazis dropped their bombs on it. However, King's story did much more than that; it lit a fire of interest and determination in me to research all I could about him and to use that research for this book. As time went on and I discovered more and more about Edward King and his life, I was at first puzzled and then angry, because the more I found out about him, the bigger the enigma got, raising more questions than answers.

What I have found out about Edward King has been a revelation to me and well worth the hours of research. Not just because of his influence on Vincent van Gogh; his exhibitions in all the major art galleries; his entries in the world's most prestigious art dictionaries; his beautiful haunting paintings of the bombed buildings of Old Portsmouth. It was his contributions to the most influential magazines in the world at a time of great social change that made him stand out for me.

The *Illustrated London News*, *The Graphic*, *Punch* and *Pall Mall* were great messengers of this social change, and like their modern counterparts, their cartoons and illustrations could, and did, make wounding political points. King's contributions to these magazines, of which I have a dozen or so copies, are the best of some of the artfully scathing comments on this new wealth and industrialisation that these publications have made. The few that I have included in this monograph illustrate the 'great divide' between the proletariat and the bourgeoisie in Victorian England.

The years that King spent in the asylum were a tragedy, not only for Edward himself but also for art, because I feel certain that if he had been able to reach his full potential he could have been as prominent in the art world as any of his contemporaries such as Sickert, Sisley, Whistler, or even, dare I suggest it, Monet? However, I have been able to demonstrate that even though he was deprived of stimulus as an artist, and there is no doubt that he became institutionalised, he was still able to beat the system and continue his painting.

The most personally felt emotion of this whole enigma of Edward King is the deep sadness I have felt for him. Throughout all my research I have tried to understand why he was perceived to be so 'dangerous' that he had to have an 'attendant' with him for almost all of his incarceration. It was only in his last few years that he was allowed the freedom to go about his painting unsupervised.

In all the letters I have read about Edward King, from former staff of the hospital, from many of his friends and from the local people in the Milton area who met and talked to him on a day-to-day basis, not one has contradicted Mary Greenwood in that,

> *I found him a most loveable, eccentric gentleman, who could talk lucidly and graphically ... He was considered genteel and quite harmless.*[21]

Or as Frank Thomas put it,

> *He was truly a person not to be associated with, or confined in a lunatic asylum. He was one of us; the residents of Milton Locks had every respect for the dear old chap.*[22]

> *I look back on King with a great deal of affection really, because he was a nice old man.*[23]

Frank Bloxham's abiding memory of Edward King.

However it was in Eleanor Traynor's long and detailed letter in the City Records Office that I found the most moving tributes to King, so much so that I have included her letter in full in my appendices section.

[21] Ibid. Goffman Asylum page 171

[22] Ibid. Goffman, Asylum, page 162

[23] Ibid. Goffman, Asylum, page 163

Eleanor Traynor thought very highly of Edward King and from amongst her many comments I have picked out just one, that to me, epitomises my own impression of him,

I was, and always will be, very grateful for having known him as I learnt a great deal from him, with all his personal grief and suffering his love of beauty remained; he was a work of art himself.[24]

So why was Edward King placed in The Portsmouth Borough Lunatic Asylum all those years ago? And why was he kept incarcerated for over twenty-five years? We have Mary Greenwood's hearsay diagnosis that he was admitted in a *Withdrawn and Unresponsive state* and Phyllis Loe's more clinical, but still hearsay diagnosis, that he was admitted with, *Profound depression, superimposed on a system of delusion, largely emanating from what he considered the origin of the world, and the contents of the Bible.* Then we have Dr. Beaton, King's supposed family friend, and his very professional and clinical diagnosis that *He was as mad as a hatter.*

What a lot of mumbo jumbo it all appears to be.

Edward King and his wife Emilie were living, as far as we know, a happy and prosperous life in East Molesey where King was a respected member of the

---

[24] Frank Thompson, 17 July 1984, Letter, Museum Records Office

community and a Justice of the Peace. Then a great disaster strikes his family, Emilie has to be admitted to Horton Hospital. Why? We do not know, although it is suggested in some of the Museum Records Office correspondence about Edward King that she was admitted to an asylum and was mentally ill and died there of Consumption. As Horton was and still is a General Hospital with perhaps a mental health ward or facility, which was quite common in those days, I am inclined to believe that Emilie was admitted and treated for Consumption, (Tuberculosis). Her subsequent death in the hospital at the latter end of 1926 must have driven King to despair; he would have been grief stricken, possibly inconsolable. He loved his wife very much, of that there is no doubt, as there are many references to this in the letters of his friends and acquaintances. *He always called her 'lovie'*, says Mary Greenwood.

In trying to understand the events leading up to King's brief incarceration in the same hospital where his wife died, it is necessary to resort to conjecture. It is possible that Edward was by his wife's side when she died, or at least was called to her bedside shortly afterwards. He would have been inconsolable, distraught and may have had to be admitted to be *kept under observation*, perhaps to prevent him harming himself. That King had some kind of breakdown is not in doubt and is perfectly understandable considering the circumstances.

These traumatic events, coupled with his incarceration in a lunatic asylum, makes it quite easy to understand King's vituperative outpourings against God and Society.

Only those who knew the hospital in those days when anyone could be confined on a whim of a relative and doctors. He spoke very bitterly about his daughter and Dr. Beaton, as he felt that after his wife's death, and he obviously loved his wife, that his daughter just wanted him out of the way to posses his material wealth and that Dr. Beaton conspired to help her do this. He was never, to my knowledge, visited by his daughter, and would walk past Dr. Beaton without speaking to him, not a word to acknowledge he knew him at all. He was a very genteel, intelligent man, he was very bitter about being where he was, and he felt totally degraded. He hated being shut away, ordered about with the loss of dignity and privacy such people as himself were subjected to and by those he felt, and quite rightly so, were less able than himself. He was a dear old man who was very lonely, bitterly disappointed and disillusioned in life, feeling very sadly let down and betrayed by those he loved and trusted.

One must remember that years ago the staff of mental institutions were not always of the highest calibre, some good people, many more like the mental patients than the patients themselves. Mental illnesses were still looked upon by many as something evil (the casting out of the devil into the swine), The sins of The Father, the result of a sinful life. Treatment of mental patients was a very hit and miss thing, little was known about the illnesses and still little than enough is known today.

Eleanor Traynor Letter. (See full transcript in Appendix)

Would it be too cynical of me to suggest that the hospital may have been trying to protect an investment, because the hospital authorities did sell King's work? In the King file in the City Records Office, there is a letter from a Mr. Bishop who wrote that his father had bought, at a hospital fête, two paintings by King. These were two complementary works, *Poplars With Haystacks*, oils on cardboard, were bought for £5 each. Mr. Bishop's father was a City Councillor, who was also on the Board of Governors of the hospital. Of course, it may well be that the authorities would have used any funds generated by the sale of King's paintings for his benefit because by this time, King's status had been changed from a private patient to that of a National Health Service one, and he may have been expected to *contribute* to his upkeep by the sale of his paintings.

The aspirations of Edward King, which formed him as an artist and as a musician in the late 1800s and early 1900s were brought to fullness in the 1940s when, as an old man working on his own, he produced his Blitz paintings. All through this period of his life he was intense and humble about his work, he gave most of it away in his later years and his greatness as an artist is in this humility. Edward King's sure instinct for form, his grace, which only goes with strength of conception, his execution of his drawings alone are enough to mark him as one of our most versatile all-round artists of that century.

I feel this quote, from a speech given by E A Carrick, (graphic artist and set designer) to the Royal Society of Arts on the 24 March 1950, is very relevant to Edward King as it was made only a year before King's death.

> *The true artist, when finally developed, becomes a teacher and a prophet to his race, whether he knows it or not. Poetry and painting, music, drama, sculpture and architecture depict emotions which, by a process of mental contagion, generate sympathetically other emotions and teach men to feel ideas which they could not comprehend in their abstract form.*

The most poignant moment for me in all my revisions and editing of this work, was when I suddenly realised that in all the research I did about Edward King's years in the asylum in Portsmouth there was no mention of his music, and I was reminded of his daughter Una's and Mary Greenwood's reminiscences of Edward,

> *All his life his two talents, painting and music pulled against each other.*

After a days painting I would eat bread and cheese, and taking up my violin I would stand back and examine my picture, playing gently the while.

Another enigma in the story of Edward King that needs to be resolved.

Finally, this Peter Gay quote about the Impressionists could have been written with Edward King in mind, more so if read in context with the piece from Eleanor P Traynor's letter.

His views on God and religion. His views on life. He wrote about human beings saying that God showed us what we were basically like when He brought us into the world next to the excretory system. Yet he had this wonderful sense of oneness with nature, the trees, grass, flowers, sea, stones, all things of natural beauty. He loved music; these things flowed with colour in his mind.

Romantics or not, articulate or not, these painters were imbued with the religion of Nature. Some among the best of them uncomfortable with theologies or metaphysics were content with lovingly depicting reality. John Constable's aphorism, 'Painting is another word for feeling', has been much quoted, but the feeling he meant was essentially to make visible the abiding affection for the scenes he had known from his youth, the lovely hills and valleys, sunlight and shade and clouds.[25]

---

[25] Ibid. Goffman, Asylum, page173

Eleanor P Traynor, retired Warden, The Hostel for the Care and Resettlement of Prisoners, Winchester, August 1984.

[The bold italics are to show underlined parts of the original text]

I first met Edward King when I went to work in the Occupational Therapy at St. James Hospital in January 1948. We remained friends until his death in 1951.

Only those who knew the hospital in those days when anyone could be confined on a whim of a relative and doctors, will appreciate the torment to someone of Edward King's sensitive, intelligent mind.

*I was a teenager having just come from the Hospital for Sick Children at Great Ormond Street after my initial examinations. Such things as occupations and occupational therapy for what was termed, **old chronico**, was in its infancy.*

*As one who is Home Office Certificated in Child Care with great experience, I look back in horror at the attitude to those confined as mentally sick and **Thank God** with all my heart that in this day and age we hope someone like Edward King be in a home for the elderly, **respected** for what he was in life.*

Edward King was a small, weathered, bent old gentleman,

*white hair and a pair of metal rimmed spectacles with thick glass through which his very blue eyes carefully **studied** and **weighed up** all he saw. He had a large growth under his chin about which he was **very** conscious. Nowadays even as a mental patient which **I never** considered he was, would have been removed.*

*He always wore a **shabby** raincoat and tweed coat, such as supplied to patients who were allowed out, and a very worn pair of boots.*

***Hail, rain** and **snow** he would daily shuffle from Pink Villa [by now King was no longer a private patient] where he resided along the hospital road past two other villas, **out** of the hospital grounds to the beach on Langstone Harbour. There he would sit and paint until it was time to shuffle back for a meal. There was a shack on the beach close to the houseboat where a Sister (Worrell?) from one of the hospital Villas lived. The people who owned the shack allowed Edward King to leave his **many** paintings there and there **were very many**.*

*He used to paint on **anything** he could **find** mostly pieces of wood and three ply, much of which I supplied to him from my father's business since materials were in short supply in those days.*

During my daily rounds at the hospital I always met Edward King and walked with him. As we got to know each other and became friends he gradually told me all about himself and his life. Often after work and during the week I would walk down to the beach and sit talking to him while he painted. **He was a very genteel, intelligent man** *who for his day and age held what would have been considered* **very controversial**, *even blasphemous views. He was an expert on the bible and could quote it from start to finish holding radical views on various things. We spent hours talking. He was* **very bitter** *about being where he was and he felt totally degraded. He hated being shut away, ordered about with the* **loss** *of dignity and privacy such people as himself were subjected* **to and by those** *he felt, and quite rightly so, were less able than himself.*

He spoke **very bitterly** *about his daughter and Dr. Beaton, as he felt that after his wife's death, and he* **obviously loved his wife**, *that his daughter just wanted him* **out of the way** *to possess his material wealth that Dr. Beaton conspired to help her do this. He was never to my knowledge visited by his daughter and would walk past Dr. Beaton without speaking to him, not a word to acknowledge he knew him at all.*

He told me that owing to the war he was bought canvasses and paints and allowed out to paint the bombed areas of Portsmouth. During these times he had **many experiences** *to tell of raids and bombings* **while he was actually working**. *He had several lucky escapes.*

In the days when I knew him again he said that he was

supplied with any materials which he wanted for his bomb paintings and that he was allowed as much freedom as he wanted to do these. I remember searching to get paints and brushes for him, as no one would get him any. He asked often.

He wrote a book, which he gave me since he felt that if the hospital saw the book and all it contained, it would be taken away and destroyed. I let a vicar borrow the book and am hoping to get it back. The book contained much of what I have written. His views on God and religion. His views on life. He wrote about human beings saying that God showed us what we were basically like when He brought us into the world next to the excretory system.

Yet he had this wonderful sense of oneness with nature, the trees, grass, flowers, sea, stones, all things of natural beauty. He loved music; these things flowed with colour in his mind.

He was a kind, gentle old man, I see him now sitting by the sea on an icy cold day, a perpetual drop almost frozen on the end of his nose, his old, frozen withered hands, covered only with the mittens my mother had knitted for him, the fingers holding one of the well worn brushes, a piece of three ply balanced on his easel and a board with an assortment of all kinds and bits of paint.

Many used to watch him paint; he was a well-known figure on the beach. He knew that many used to laugh at him but in truth he was a very kind, dear old man who was very lonely, bitterly disappointed and disillusioned in life feeling very sadly let down and betrayed by those he loved and trusted. It would not happen we hope today.

I was and always will be very grateful for having known him as I learnt a great deal from him, with all his personal grief and suffering his love of beauty remained; he was a work of art himself.

Alas nowadays he could have expressed his views on the bible and other aspects of life without being considered a heretic, a lunatic. He was neither. I wonder what he would he think about this exhibition, [Portsmouth; Home Front 1984] he gave his paintings away to give, often, the less fortunate some pleasure and colour in life. I doubt many of those who received his paintings even knew his name and that many paintings lie rotten and eaten with woodworm, a sad loss to all. A far greater loss than the forthcoming closure of St. James Hospital which I am sure Edward King would rejoice to Know. [The expected closure never took place]

Edward King was an intellectual who had studied greatly and held in fact views that would be accepted and approved off by today's younger generation. The Bishop of Durham expressed the sort of views that King himself might have expressed. Some have held up their hands in horror and chanted 'throw him out' but no one has suggested he be shut away because of mental deterioration.

Edward had a fantastic memory and talked quite rationally with those he could communicate and had something in common with.

One must remember that years ago the staff of mental institutions were not always of the highest calibre, some good people, many more like the mental patients than the patients themselves. Mental illnesses were still looked upon by many as something evil (the casting out of the devil into the swine), The sins of the Father, the result of a sinful life. I doubt that many of the staff would have heard of Proust, Voltaire, Bach or Mozart. Treatment of mental patients was a very hit and miss thing, little was known about the illnesses and still little than enough is known today but at least we hope that patients are afforded the respect that every human being is entitled to.

*Edward King was well aware of these and had his own theories, he often said if he were younger he would do more about these things. He also used to say what good would it be if he tried to escape he would be brought back, sedated and locked in a ward or room. He often painted the hospital washing parties controlled by male nurses. One might hope some of those paintings still exist for the expressed the faces of the inmates so wonderfully. One I remember so well, of a one-time sailor who had been torpedoed while aboard a ship and as a result had a complete breakdown. I recall the man well, a very fine looking blonde man no more than in his early twenties, a **zombie**.*

Edward's painting of him on the hospital farm guarded by nurse expressed the look of acceptance and the very **hopelessness** *on his face and the acceptance and hopelessness Edward himself had felt for so long.*

He **seldom** *painted people as he said it had been many years since he felt he had much in common with the majority of them. He mostly kept himself to himself and held his own counsel. I myself was looked upon by many as an oddity for bothering to talk to and make friends with Edward or any other inmate, the* **attitude** *then was so different. I write these things to give you some idea of what his life was like, his pictures of the bombed war torn city expressed his feelings for man's contempt of man, man's destruction of man. In his paintings the created his sea scenes depicted his escape, the sea was something that man could not control, the things of nature that refused to be destroyed by man, flowers growing on a bombed site.*

I would appeal to anyone who has even a fragment of Edward's paintings to bring them to the museum; they express life as Edward felt it to the end. His innermost feelings of beauty, loneliness, strength and that which was greater than man. The things he felt that man did not appreciate or understand. I would willingly have had Edward King to live with me and cared for him. His feeling of disgust for man were not directed at man in general but at those he felt should have known better and shown greater understanding and responsibility to their fellow human beings.

Dr. Beaton was a personal family friend, he knew him quite well. I also knew many of the doctors at that time practicing at St. James and did in fact stay with several of them as a guest in their homes. They also visited my home. This gave me the opportunity of learning about their attitudes to mental illnesses and that, which was thought to be abnormal.

*

King's Gallery Valuations

Edward King's *The Workman's Train*

Van Gogh's Final Study for *The Potato Eaters*

Some Gallery Valuations of King's work:

Royal Society of British Artists, 1824-1893
1886   (422) *Village Street* £15 15s (Fifteen Guineas)
1887   (294) *The Village Street South Harting* £100-0s-0p
1888   (62) *A Summer Afternoon* £200-0s-0p
1889   (339) *Amy, Daughter of JJ Harcourt Esq.* (not for sale)[26]

Works not valued, exhibition only
1888   (9) *Sympathy*
        (14) *A Heavy Load*
1889   (10)*'and all the air a solemn stillness holds'*
1910   (206) *South Rustington Church*
        (252) *The Canal, Lalngollen, (Autumn Sunshine)*
1911   (223) *Springwell Lock, Richmansworth 2*

Cheltenham Gallery and Museum
1909   (16) *Avenue at Cojé, France* £30.0s.0
1914   (48) *A Surrey Farm* £200.0s.0p

---

[26] Works Exhibited at the Royal Society of British Artists, 1824-1893. 1975 Antique Collectors Club Research Project, Compiled by Jane Johnson Baron Publishing, Suffolk, vol.1. p.269

Edward King's Art Dictionary Entries

Bénézit, E. 1966, *Dictionnaire des Peintres, Sculpteurs, Dessinatuers et Graveurs*, Libraire Grand, Paris

Checklist of British Artists in the Witt Library, 1991, Courtauld Institute of Art, London

Graves, Algernon F.S.A. 1901, *Dictionary of Artists Who Have Exhibited Works in the Principle London Exhibitions From 1760 to 1893*, Kingsmead Reprints, Bath

Houfe, Simon. 1978, *The Dictionary of 19th Century British Book Illustrators*, Antique Collectors Club, Baron Publishing, Suffolk

Johnson & Greutzer. 1976, *Dictionary of British Artists 1880-1940*, Antique Collectors Club, (as above)

Johnson, Jane. 1973, *Works Exhibited at the Royal Society of British Artists 1824-1893*, Antique Collectors Club, (as above)

The Pall Mall Magazine, vol. Five, 1893, Edward King five Illustrations.

Stewart & Cutten. 1988, *The Dictionary of Portrait Painters*, Antique Collectors Club, (as above)

The Royal Academy Exhibitions 1905-1970 vol.1V, 1979, EP Publications Ltd. Yorkshire

Water, Grant. 1974, *Dictionary of British Artists 1900-1950*, Eastbourne Fine Art Publishing, Eastbourne

Wood, Christopher. 1981, *The Dictionary of Victorian Painters*, Antique Collectors Club, (as above)

Works Exhibited at the Royal Society of British Artists, 1824-1893. 1975 Antique Collectors Club Research Project, Compiled by Jane Johnson, (as above)

Appendix

(a) Lori Misura e-mail

(b) Elaine Hart e-mail

(c) Barbara Thompson e-mail

(d) Manchester Art Gallery Letter

(e) Edward King's Art Dictionary Entries

(f) Edward King's Exhibitions

(g) Edward King's Royal Academy Exhibitions

(h) Gallery valuations of King's work

(i) Edward King Painting Offered for Sale at Sotheby's

(j) Edward King's Lithographs in the Witt Library

(k) List of Edward King's Blitz paintings

(l) Letter from Edward King's daughter, Una

(m) Friends and Patrons

(n) St James' Letter

(o) Frank Thompson Letter

(p) Evening News 22 July 1942 Photo of King

(q) Margaret Beddoes Article about King

(r) Eleanor P. Traynor Letter